AWESOME ATHLETES

CAL RIPKEN, JR.

Paul Joseph
ABDO & Daughters

Published by Abdo & Daughters, 4940 Viking Drive, Suite 622, Edina, Minnesota 55435.

Copyright © 1997 by Abdo Consulting Group, Inc., Pentagon Tower, P.O. Box 36036, Minneapolis, Minnesota 55435 USA. International copyrights reserved in all countries. No part of this book may be reproduced in any form without written permission from the publisher.

Printed in the United States.

Cover and Interior Photo credits: Wide World Photos
Allsport USA

Edited by Kal Gronvall

Library of Congress Cataloging-in-Publication Data

Joseph, Paul, 1970-
Cal Ripken, Jr. / Paul Joseph.
    p. cm. — (Awesome athletes)
Includes index.
Summary: A biography of the Baltimore Orioles' shortstop who earned the nickname Iron Man in 1995 when he broke Lou Gehrig's record for most games played in a row.
ISBN 1-56239-638-2
1. Ripken, Cal, 1960- —Juvenile literature. 2. Baseball players—United States—Biography—Juvenile literature. 3. Baltimore Orioles (Baseball team)—Juvenile literature. [1. Ripken, Cal, 1960- . 2. Baseball players.] I. Title. II . Series.
GV865.R47J67 1997
796.357'092—dc20
[B]   96-16087
                                                                      CIP
                                                                       AC

Contents

Iron Man

Lou Gehrig set one of the most amazing **records** in baseball—actually in any sport. He played in 2,130 baseball games in a row.

Most **experts** believed that Gehrig's record would never be broken, considering it has stood since 1939. But then Cal Ripken, Jr., came along.

On September 6, 1995, Cal tied Gehrig's record, and he also hit a **home run** in that game. The next night the impossible happened: Cal played in his 2,131st game— breaking the record that most people felt would never be broken.

Cal has always loved the game of baseball. As a child he watched his dad play **professional baseball**. He learned a lot about the game by watching his dad and his dad's team. Then he would go out and practice what he had seen.

Besides the unbelievable **record** of not missing a game since May 30, 1982, Cal has also done other great things in his baseball career, including winning a **World Series**.

Through hard work, Cal has earned for himself the nickname "Iron Man." He is truly in a class of his own.

Cal Ripken, Jr., rounds third after hitting a home run while playing in his record-tying 2,130th consecutive game.

A Family Game

Cal Ripken, Jr., was born on August 24, 1960, in Havre de Grace, Maryland, to Cal and Vi Ripken. His father was a long way away, playing **minor league** baseball, in Topeka, Kansas. This was not unusual as Cal, Sr., was gone every summer while Cal, Jr., was growing up, either playing or coaching baseball.

Cal, Jr., has two brothers, Fred and Billy, and one sister, Ellen. All were very **athletic** but they didn't just get their athletic ability from their father. Their mother Vi was a very good softball player in high school and helped teach them the game of baseball when their father was gone.

During the summers the whole family would be together. Vi would pack up all the kids and head to wherever Cal, Sr., was playing or coaching.

This was great for the Ripken kids, especially Cal, who had such a love for the game. When the other kids were running around and playing, Cal would be right next to the fence watching the game. He would take notes and ask his father why someone did this, or why he did that, or why a player bunted in a certain situation. His dad would always answer every question so Cal could learn.

His father told his mother that Cal asked better questions than the **reporters** did. By the time Cal was 10 years old he knew the game inside and out.

From left to right: Cal, Jr., Cal, Sr., and Billy Ripken.

Aberdeen High School Star

Cal played **Little League** growing up, and was by far the best player in the league. Many thought the credit should go to his father because he was a **professional baseball** player. But it was actually his mother who should have received most of the credit, for she always pitched to him and took him to the games. He called her "his number one **fan**."

Still Cal's favorite part of the summer was going to see his father play baseball. Cal would take batting practice with the players and take ground balls at **shortstop**. More important, he continued to watch, ask questions, and learn more about the game.

By the time Cal started Aberdeen High School he knew the game very well—but he played it even better. He knew that he wanted to make baseball his career. When he was given an assignment to write down what he wanted to be when he grew up, he wrote that he wanted to be a **professional baseball** player!

By this time Cal's father was a coach with the Baltimore Orioles **Major League** Baseball team. Cal would often go to Memorial Stadium, where the Orioles played, to practice with the "big leaguers." The players were very impressed with Cal. At 15 years old, Cal was hitting balls out of the park. And he still continued to ask questions about the game. Cal knew that he had talent, but so did a lot of players. Cal wanted to know the game well enough that he could play it by **instinct**.

Cal started his high school baseball career as a five-foot-seven-inch, 125-pound infielder. He made the **varsity** team his first year and was very good. His coach couldn't believe how good he was at the **fundamentals** of the game and how well he knew the game.

Cal was the star pitcher and **shortstop**. More important, though, he led the team in every offensive category, from **home runs** to hits, to **RBIs**, and even to **stolen bases**.

Cal was the star of the team, but the team didn't do too well during Cal's first few years. But by the time Cal was a senior in high school, people knew him and they knew Aberdeen High School.

By this time Cal was six feet, two inches tall and weighed 175 pounds. As a pitcher he led his team to the state championship game by pitching 60 innings during the season, and striking out 100 batters. He also batted .492 and drove in 29 runs in 20 games.

In the Maryland State Championship game he allowed only 2 hits and struck out 17. He also had key hits that brought in runs. Cal and his team were State Champions.

Cal is Drafted

Scouts from many **Major League** teams came to watch Cal play in high school. They all knew that he could make it in the major leagues. There was only one problem. They didn't know if they should **draft** him for his pitching or for his play at **shortstop**.

As a pitcher Cal could throw the ball more than 80 miles per hour and had great control. As a shortstop he had an excellent arm and made very few **errors**. But what the scouts liked was that he could hit. As a pitcher he might never get to hit.

Cal made the decision himself. He made it clear that he wouldn't play for a team that wanted him as a pitcher. Cal wanted to play every day and to be able to hit. As a pitcher he might play only every third or fourth game.

Colleges also wanted Cal to go to their schools and play baseball. Cal was an excellent student, with an A-average, but he knew that he always wanted to play

professional baseball, and now he had his chance. So Cal chose to become a professional baseball player directly out of high school rather than go to college to play college ball.

Cal was the 42nd player chosen in the 1978 **draft**—by none other than his favorite team, the Baltimore Orioles. Cal made it to professional baseball, and he was going to play for a team that he watched while he was growing up. Things couldn't have turned out much better, but it was only the beginning of the good things for Cal.

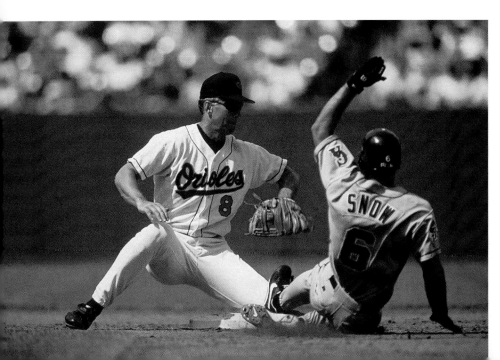

Cal Ripken, Jr., (8) attempts to make a play at second base.

Playing in the Minors

Cal quickly signed his first pro **contract** and went to Bluefield, West Virginia, where he played for the Orioles' **minor league** team.

In Cal's first season he played mostly **shortstop**, although at times he would play third base. In his second year in the minors he played third base for the entire season. The Orioles thought that, in the long run, third base would be Cal's best position.

During his first two seasons in the minors Cal was not playing well. He was still trying to adjust to this new lifestyle of living on the road and playing baseball every day—sometimes twice a day.

In 1980, his third season, Cal led his team with 25 **home runs**. He was beginning to live up to everyone's expectations.

Cal Ripken, Sr., congratulates his son for a home run.

1960	1976	1978	1981
Born August 24 in Havre de Grace, Maryland.	Pitches for Aberdeen High School.	Drafted by the Baltimore Orioles and sent to the minor leagues.	Joins the Baltimore Orioles' Major League team.

How Awesome Is He?

Here is the list of the Major League's all-time consecutive-games-played streaks:

Player	Position	Games
Cal Ripken, Jr.	**Shortstop**	**2,131***
Lou Gehrig	First base	2,130
Everett Scott	Shortstop	1,307
Steve Garvey	First base	1,207
Billy Williams	Left field	1,117
Joe Sewell	Shortstop	1,103
Stan Musial	Outfield/ First base	895

*the streak continues. . .

CAL RIPKEN, JR.

TEAM: BALTIMORE ORIOLES
NUMBER: 8
POSITION: SHORTSTOP
HEIGHT: 6 FEET 4 INCHES
WEIGHT: 225 LBS.

1982	1983	1991	1995
Named the AL Rookie of the Year.	Named AL MVP. Leads Orioles to a World Series Championship.	Named All-Star MVP and AL MVP.	Breaks Lou Gehrig's consecutive-games-played streak.

- 1982 AL Rookie of the Year
- 2-Time AL MVP
- World Series Champ, 1983
- 13-Time All-Star Selection
- Record-95 Straight Errorless Games in 1990
- 2-Time Gold Glove Winner
- Holder of the Longest Consecutive-Games-Played Streak in Professional Sports

Highlights

Cal's First Historic Moment

By 1981, Cal had made it to the Orioles' top **minor league** team, the Rochester Red Wings. During that season Cal played in a **historic** game against the Pawtucket Red Sox.

The score was tied 1-1 after nine innings—which meant extra innings. There turned out to be lots and lots of extra innings. In the 21st inning the Red Wings scored a run but the Red Sox came back and tied the game again.

Neither team scored again until the bottom of the 33rd inning! The Red Sox finally won the longest game in the history of organized baseball.

Cal played every inning of that game, batting 13 times. His iron man performance in that game was a sign of things to come. He finished that season with 23 **home runs** and was the league's **Rookie of the Year**.

Cal Makes
the Majors

Although Cal was named **Rookie of the Year** in the minors, he didn't get a chance to finish the season there. On August 8, 1981, Cal was called up to play in the **Major Leagues** with the Baltimore Orioles.

Cal now fulfilled his dream of playing in the Major Leagues. He also would now get to see his dad every day; Cal, Sr., was the third base coach.

In Cal's first game as a Major Leaguer he scored the winning run. He played both **shortstop** and third base his first season, but mainly he sat on the bench and watched.

Since he had played in so few games his first season he was still considered a **rookie** when the next season began.

The Streak Begins

The 1982 season will be remembered as "the season the streak began."

On May 29, Cal sat out the second game of a **double header** against Toronto. That was the last game in which Cal didn't play. The next day he was back in the lineup to begin an incredible streak that most say will never be broken.

Cal began the season at third base, but on July 1, he was back at the position he loved: **shortstop**. Cal played great **defense** that year, and offensively he ended the year with 28 **home runs** and 93 **RBIs**. He was also chosen **Rookie of the Year**.

Opposite page: Orioles third base
coach Cal Ripken, Sr., (L) with his son
Cal Ripken, Jr.

What A Year!

Cal had an excellent **rookie** year, but the next year he performed even better. In fact, the whole team played improved ball with Cal in the lineup.

The Orioles won the American League East and easily captured the American League pennant by beating the Chicago White Sox in a best of five series, three games to one.

They were now in the **World Series**, getting ready to play the Philadelphia Phillies. Cal had dreamed of playing in the World Series many times as a youngster. He just couldn't believe it was finally coming true.

The Orioles were leading three games to one. They needed one more win to be World Champions. The Orioles were ahead 5-0 in the bottom of the ninth, with two outs, when the Phillies' Gary Maddox hit a line drive to Cal. After catching the liner, Cal slammed the ball to the ground and ran to his pitcher. Cal and the Orioles were winners of the World Series!

In addition to the **World Series** victory, Cal was also named the season's **Most Valuable Player (MVP)**. He finished the year batting .318, with 27 **home runs**, and 102 **RBIs**. What a year!

Cal Ripken collides with teammate Todd Cruz during the 1983 World Series.

The Streak Continues

After that great year in 1983, the Baltimore Orioles did not have much luck. One thing remained the same, though. And that was Cal Ripken, Jr., at **shortstop**.

Between winning a **World Series** in 1983 and breaking Lou Gehrig's **record** in 1995, Cal continued to play and play—never missing a game!

In every one of those years he was an **All-Star**. In 1991, he was the All-Star Game's **MVP** and the league's MVP. He received the league MVP by batting .323, smashing 34 **home runs**, and knocking in 114 **RBIs**.

In 1987 and 1988, Cal was coached by his father, who was named manager of the Orioles. He was also able to play alongside his brother, Billy, who was now the second baseman. It didn't last long, though. After another bad season for the Orioles, Cal, Sr., was fired as manager and went back to coaching third base. Billy was let go after the 1992 season.

But all these disappointments never stopped Cal from playing. His streak continued. And then on Wednesday, September 6, 1995, Cal tied the greatest **record** in all of sports—Lou Gehrig's 2,130-games-played streak.

He did it in the regular Cal Ripken style, hitting a **home run** and getting three hits, as the Orioles won 8-0.

Cal receives an award for the longest consecutive-games-played streak in professional sports.

Cal Makes History

The following night Cal prepared to break the longest playing streak in any sport. Before the game he gave many interviews and had visits from all kinds of people, including President Bill Clinton. Finally, it was game time. When Cal came to bat for the first time, leading off the second inning, the sellout crowd of 46,272 gave him a 45-second standing **ovation**. In the fourth inning, Cal hit a game-winning **home run** that carried the Orioles to a 4-2 victory.

In the fifth inning, at 9:21 P.M., the game became official. Cal Ripken, Jr., had officially broken Lou Gehrig's **record**. The **fans** at Camden Yards, joined by players from both teams and the umpires, erupted in a 22-minute standing ovation!

Cal, a very **modest** man, was coaxed out of the dugout by his teammates. He waved his left hand, then his right, his left again and remained in front of the dugout for two minutes to allow the fans to get their fill. But when the cheering didn't stop, Ripken reappeared and waved to the crowd three more times, swinging both hands upward in unison.

The cheering wouldn't stop. Cal then got out of the dugout and began trotting down the right-field foul line, waving at the fans. He then cut across the outfield and high-fived a few ushers who were standing on the warning track. A few hands reached out of the bleachers and he slapped those. Somebody threw a cap on the field and he tossed it back.

Cal continued into left field, and now he was slowing down, slapping many more hands. The walk continued along the left-field stands with more handshakes and hugs. He stopped near the Orioles' dugout to kiss his wife, his son, and his daughter, and then he disappeared into the dugout, where he grabbed a towel to wipe the sweat from his face.

After the game, a postgame **ceremony** was held in Cal's honor. Cal walked up to the microphone and said, "Tonight I stand here, overwhelmed, as my name is linked with the great and courageous Lou Gehrig. I'm truly humbled to have our names spoken in the same breath.   As I grew up here, I not only had dreams of being a big-league ballplayer, but of being a Baltimore Oriole. As a boy and a **fan**, I know how passionate we feel about baseball, and the Orioles and I have benefited as a player for that passion. I want to thank you from the bottom of my heart. This is the greatest place to play.

"This year has been unbelievable. I have been cheered in ballparks all over the country. . . I give my thanks to baseball fans everywhere."

He ended his speech in typical Cal style, by showing his love for the game and for his All-American work ethic: "Whether your name is Gehrig or Ripken, or that of some youngster who picks up his bat or puts on his glove, you are challenged by the game of baseball to do your very best, day in and day out. And that's all that I've ever tried to do."

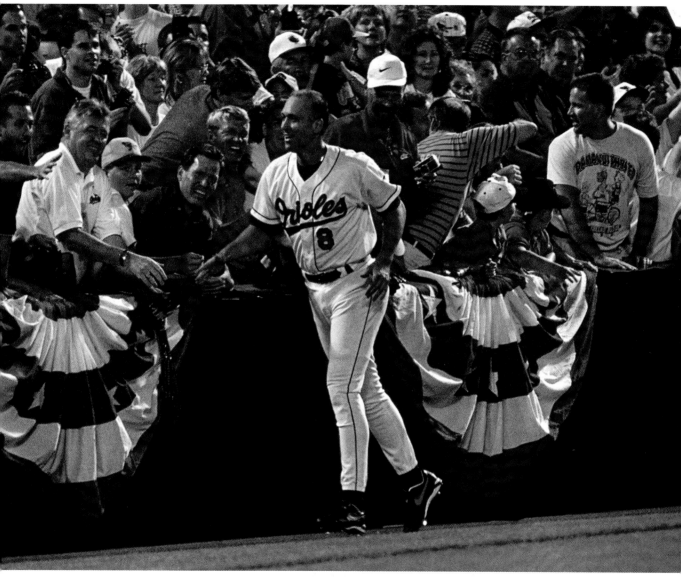

Cal Ripken laps Camden Yards to the thrill of his fans.

GLOSSARY

All-Star - A player who is voted by fans as the best player at one position in a given year.

athletic - Someone who is talented at sports.

ceremony - A special time when people celebrate a special event.

contract - A legal document signed by players that determines their pay and how many years they will play for a particular team.

defense - The baseball team on the field that tries to get the offense out.

double header - Playing two baseball games in the same day, one after the other.

draft - An event during which Major League Baseball teams choose high school or college players.

error - When someone on the defense makes a catching or throwing mistake.

expert - Someone who knows the game of baseball very well.

fans - People who cheer for their favorite players and team.

fundamentals - The most important and basic baseball skills.

historic - A famous or important event in history that rarely takes place or has never taken place before.

hit - When the batter hits the ball and reaches base safely without the aid of an error.

home run - When a batter hits the ball over the outfield fence, scoring everyone on the bases as well as the batter.

instinct - A natural way of reacting to something without thinking about it.

Little League - A baseball league for children 9 to 12 years old.

Major League - The highest ranking of professional baseball teams in the world, consisting of the American and National Leagues.

minor league - The three classes and rookie league of professional baseball at levels below the Major League.

modest - Not thinking too highly of oneself.

Most Valuable Player (MVP) - An award given to the best player in the Major League, All-Star Game, or World Series.

offense - The baseball team at-bat.

ovation - Standing, clapping, and cheering for something special a person has done.

professional baseball - A baseball league in which players get paid to play.

RBI - Runs Batted In. Players receive an RBI for each run that scores on their hits.

record - The best that has ever been done in a certain event.

reporters - People who gather and report news for a newspaper, magazine, radio, or television station.

rookie - A first-year player in a sport.

Rookie of the Year - An award honoring the best rookie player.

scouts - People who determine if amateur athletes have the talent to become professional.

shortstop - The position between second and third base that fields the most ground balls during a baseball game.

stolen base - When a base runner advances to the next base while the pitcher throws a pitch.

varsity - The best team in a high school sport.

World Series - The championship of Major League Baseball played between the National and American League champions.

Index